NOMAR GARCIAPARRA

CARLTON FISK

WADE BOGGS

LEFTY GROVE

PEDRO MARTINEZ

CY YOUNG

BABE RUTH

ROGER CLEMENS

TED WILLIAMS

JIM RICE

MANNY RAMIREZ

CARL YASTRZEMSKI

THE HISTORY OF THE

BOSTON RED SOX

AARON FRISCH

CREATIVE 🍎 EDUCATION

Published by Creative Education, 123 South Broad Street, Mankato, MN 56001

Creative Education is an imprint of The Creative Company.

Designed by Rita Marshall.

Photographs by AllSport (Jeff Gross, Jed Jacobsohn, Rick Stewart), Associated Press/Wide World

Photos, Anthony Neste, Sports Gallery (David Drapkin), SportsChrome (Rob Tringali Jr.,

Bryan Yablonsky)

Library of Congress Cataloging-in-Publication Data

Frisch, Aaron. The history of the Boston Red Sox / by Aaron Frisch.

p. cm. — (Baseball)   ISBN 1-58341-202-6

Summary: Highlights the key personalities and memorable games in the history of the

team that began playing in 1901 under the name Boston Pilgrims.

1. Boston Red Sox (Baseball team)—History—

Juvenile literature. [1. Boston Red Sox (Baseball team)—History.

2. Baseball—History.] I. Title. II. Baseball (Mankato, Minn.).

GV875.B62 F75 2002   796.357'64'0974461—dc21   2001047860

First Edition 9 8 7 6 5 4 3 2 1

MOST OF

THE FIRST ENGLISH COLONISTS WHO ARRIVED IN

America in the 1600s settled in the northeastern part of the country,

a region that soon came to be known as New England. At the heart

of this region is Boston, Massachusetts, which today boasts some of

America's oldest and best schools, libraries, and museums. Because

of its great array of historic institutions, Boston is sometimes referred

to as "the Hub."

Boston can lay claim to many American "firsts." It was home to

the country's first college, the first newspaper, and the first light-

house. It was fitting, therefore, that the city became home to one of

the first baseball teams in the American League (AL) in 1901.

Mixing great early success with many frustrating near-misses, that

CY YOUNG

team—the Boston Red Sox—has become an obsession among many New Englanders.

Boston's superb pitching staff posted a collective 2.12 ERA in **1904**— still the lowest in club history.

{CY, THE BABE, AND A DYNASTY} When the Red Sox were assembled in 1901, they were known as the Pilgrims, a fitting name given Boston's history and the team's role as a charter member of the AL. The Pilgrims were an instant success, winning the league championship in just their third season. Boston then beat the Pittsburgh Pirates—champions of the National League (NL)—to win the very first World Series.

Boston's first teams were built around great pitchers, and no pitcher was better than Denton "Cy" Young. Young joined the Pilgrims in 1901 at the age of 34 and played eight seasons with the team. Over the course of his amazing 21-year career, he won 511 games—a record that may never be broken (no other major-league pitcher

MO VAUGHN

Young star Babe Ruth joined Boston in **1914** and led the Sox to three titles.

BABE RUTH

has even won 400 games). His greatness is still honored today in the form of the Cy Young Award, which is given every year to the best pitcher in each league.

Young was Boston's top pitcher during those years, but hurlers Bill Dinneen, Tom Hughes, and Jesse Tannehill could be equally devastating. In 1908, yet another star pitcher, "Smokey" Joe Wood, joined the team. Behind this sensational pitching staff, Boston remained a powerhouse for its first decade.

"Smokey" Joe Wood was a terror on the mound in **1912**, going 35–4 and striking out 258 batters.

In 1912, the team—which by then had been named the Red Sox, a reference to its players' bright and nontraditional socks—moved into a new stadium called Fenway Park, which was distinguished by a green, 37-foot left-field wall that became known as the "Green Monster." The move only seemed to increase Boston's power. That season, the Red Sox topped the New York Giants to

JOE WOOD

Built in **1912**, Fenway Park has become one of the most treasured landmarks in Boston.

FENWAY PARK

win their second World Series. But the Sox didn't stop there. They rolled to World Series victories again in 1915, 1916, and 1918.

The Red Sox were sensational in **1918**, holding opponents scoreless in 26 of their 75 victories.

Leading the way in many of those victories was a new Boston star: pitcher George Herman Ruth, better known as "Babe." After dominating in the team's 1916 and 1918 World Series triumphs, Ruth asked Red Sox owner Harry Frazee to move him to the outfield

instead so he could concentrate more on hitting. Sadly for Boston fans, Ruth soon made another move—to the rival New York Yankees.

Frazee, who bought the Red Sox in 1917, made a habit of selling his best players to the Yankees to make money for his financially struggling Frazee Theatre in New York City. He quickly sold almost all of Boston's best players, including Babe Ruth. A popular legend in Boston has it that after Ruth was sold to the Yankees, he put a hex on the Red Sox to make sure they would never win a World

JIMMIE FOXX

Series without him. The "Curse of the Bambino" has indeed seemed

to haunt the team ever since.

{ONWARD WITH WILLIAMS} Thanks to Frazee's dealings,

the Yankees built a dynasty, while the Red Sox fell into a slump that

lasted nearly 20 years. The team featured some talented players during

the 1920s and early '30s, including pitcher Howard Ehmke and first baseman Earl Webb, but by 1933, the Red Sox had suffered 15 straight losing seasons.

Boston set a major-league record when four consecu- tive batters smacked triples in a **1934** game.

Things began to improve in Boston in the mid-1930s after Thomas A. Yawkey bought the team. Unlike Frazee, Yawkey brought in players instead of selling them off. Among the great players he acquired were shortstop Joe Cronin, slugging first baseman

14 Jimmie Foxx, and pitchers Wes Ferrell and Lefty Grove. The Red Sox also developed some terrific home-grown players during those years, including second baseman Bobby Doerr and outfielder Ted Williams.

When Williams joined Boston's lineup in 1939, some of his teammates laughed after looking at his skinny frame and watching his awkward base-running gallop. But Williams negated his short-comings with two things: a sweet swing and confidence. In 1941, he

JIM RICE

set one of the game's most hallowed records by posting an amazing

.406 batting average. "All I want out of life," he once said, "is that

when I walk down the street, folks will say, 'There goes the greatest

hitter who ever lived.'"

In the early 1940s, Williams and some of his teammates left

baseball to serve their country in World War II. In 1946, when the war had ended, they returned and won Boston's seventh AL pennant. Williams led a lineup of good hitters, and Dave "Boo" Ferriss led a strong pitching staff. But the Red Sox couldn't bring home a sixth world championship, losing to the St. Louis Cardinals in the World Series.

Boston failed to reach the playoffs again throughout the rest of the 1940s and '50s. As the losses mounted, Red Sox fans began to voice their frustration with the team. Through all the dark times, Williams never faltered, leading the AL in home runs in 1947 and 1949 and leading the league in batting average six different seasons. In 1960, he ended his career in style, clouting his 521st home run in his last at-bat.

{THE CLOSE CALLS CONTINUE} Just a year after Williams's retirement, a new star stepped forward to lead the Red Sox. That player was rookie left fielder Carl Yastrzemski, known to fans as

Between **1940** and **1960**, the legendary Ted Williams represented Boston in 18 All-Star Games.

17

TED WILLIAMS

simply "Yaz." Yastrzemski wasn't as tall or as powerful as Williams,

but he had a smooth left-handed swing that helped him win the AL

In **1972**, Carlton Fisk's 22 home runs and great defense earned him AL Rookie of the Year honors.

batting crown in 1963. Despite his offensive heroics,

however, the Red Sox remained near the bottom of

the standings.

Boston finally surged to life in 1967 with a 92–70

record. Yaz hit 44 home runs and drove in 121 runs

that year, but powerful first baseman George Scott and pitcher Jim

Lonborg played big roles as well. These players led the Sox to the

World Series, where they faced the St. Louis Cardinals. As had hap-

pened in 1946, the Red Sox lost to the Cardinals in seven games.

The Red Sox continued to expand their stable of new stars in

the years that followed. Catcher Carlton Fisk arrived in 1972 and was

soon joined by pitcher Luis Tiant and talented young outfielders

Fred Lynn and Jim Rice. These players led the way as Boston won

CARLTON FISK

the AL Eastern Division in 1975 (the league was divided into two

divisions in 1969) and advanced to the World Series to face the

Cincinnati Reds. Fisk hit a dramatic, extra-inning home run in game

six of the series to force a game seven, but the Reds then won

the championship.

Three years later, the Red Sox finished the season tied with the Yankees for the division lead. To determine the winner, the two

teams met in a one-game playoff at Fenway Park. Fate once again

In **1979**, Fred Lynn batted .333, becoming the seventh Boston player to win an AL batting crown.

turned cruel for Boston fans as light-hitting Yankees

shortstop Bucky Dent popped a fly ball over the

Green Monster left-field wall to give New York the

win and the division title.

In 1983, Yastrzemski retired with 3,419 career hits,

22 452 home runs, and a revered place in Red Sox history. "It's a great

accomplishment to blend power with consistency," said Hall of

Fame outfielder Frank Robinson. "When I was playing in the league,

he was the only one I considered a true superstar."

{BOGGS AND "THE ROCKET"} Taking Yastrzemski's place

as Boston's best hitter was a young third baseman named Wade

Boggs. Boggs didn't hit for power, but his amazing concentration

made him a sensational line-drive hitter. In 1983, his first season as a

FRED LYNN

Ellis Burks was one of several slugging outfielders that starred for the Sox in the **1980s**.

ELLIS BURKS

starter, Boggs led the AL in batting.

A year later, the Red Sox added another future star in young

pitcher Roger Clemens, a big right-hander from Texas.

With a blazing fastball and a nasty demeanor, Clemens

soon became known as "the Rocket." "He throws so

hard that even when you know the heat's coming you

can't hit it," said Kansas City Royals first baseman

Steve Balboni.

"The Rocket,"
Roger Clemens,
dominated
hitters as he
rolled to a
24–4 mark
during the
1986 season.

Boggs, Clemens, and Jim Rice led Boston to the AL pennant in

1986. In the World Series, the Red Sox jumped out to a three-

games-to-two lead over the New York Mets. Game six in New York

went into extra innings, but with two outs in the bottom of the 10th,

Boston led 5–3. Then, with the Sox needing only one out to become

world champions, the unthinkable happened.

As the Red Sox faithful watched in horror, Boston gave up

ROGER CLEMENS

three runs on three singles, a wild pitch, and an error by first

baseman Bill Buckner on a slow-rolling ground ball. The Mets won

the game, and two days later, they finished off the reeling Red Sox

to win the series. "That's baseball," said stunned Boston manager

John McNamara. "This game is my life, but man, it can test

you. . . . I don't think I'll get over this."

Boggs, Clemens, and outfielders Mike Greenwell and Ellis

Burks kept the Red Sox among the AL's best the next few seasons,

but the team could not get back to the World Series. | Though solid

Then, in the early 1990s, things went south. Boston | in the field,

Wade Boggs

finished last in its division in 1992 and spent the next | was better

known for

few years fighting its way back up the standings. | his uncanny

skill at

{A RED SOX RESURGENCE} By 1995, the Red | the plate.

Sox had finally regained their form. Big first baseman Mo Vaughn

emerged as one of the league's top sluggers, clouting 39 home runs

and driving in 129 runs—numbers that earned him the AL Most

Valuable Player (MVP) award. Infielder John Valentin also helped

out as the Red Sox won their division again before falling in

the playoffs.

Boston remained a force throughout the late '90s as new stars

replaced the departed Boggs and Clemens. One such star was short-

WADE BOGGS

stop Nomar Garciaparra, who led the league in hits as a rookie in 1997. Although he was amazing at the plate—winning AL batting crowns in 1999 and 2000—he was perhaps even better in the field, showing great range and a rifle arm. He also endeared himself to Sox fans with his old-fashioned hustle on the base paths.

Replacing Clemens as Boston's pitching ace was

Pedro Martinez, who joined the Red Sox after winning the 1997 NL Cy Young Award with the Montreal Expos. The Dominican Republic native was a pitching marvel, firing the ball with pinpoint accuracy and a velocity that seemed impossible for a man of his size (5-foot-11 and 170 pounds). "That little man's the best I've ever seen," said Red Sox pitcher Bret Saberhagen, himself a two-time Cy Young Award winner. "In my era, you've got Roger Clemens, Randy Johnson, Greg Maddux—but as far as I'm concerned, Pedro's the best."

JOSE VALENTIN

The Red Sox made the playoffs in 1998 and 1999 as a wild-card team. Garciaparra and Martinez led the way, but closer Tom "Flash" Gordon played a major role as well. In 1998, Gordon nailed down 46 saves, including a major-league record 43 in a row without a loss. Unfortunately, Boston could not reach the World Series either year, falling to the Cleveland Indians in 1998 and losing to the Yankees in 1999.

With 42 saves, Derek Lowe replaced the departed Tom Gordon as Boston's top reliever in **2000**.

The 2001 season was a rocky one in Boston. The team was loaded with talent—including reliever Derek Lowe and hard-hitting outfielders Carl Everett and Manny Ramirez—but injuries hindered many players, including Garciaparra and Martinez. Even though the Red Sox again finished with a winning record, manager Jimy Williams was fired late in the year. The changes continued in the off-season as new owners took over the franchise and brought in

DEREK LOWE

A three-time
Cy Young
Award winner,
Pedro
Martinez
was Boston's
top gun.

PEDRO MARTINEZ

Manny Ramirez supplied most of the Red Sox's power in **2001** with 41 home runs.

MANNY RAMIREZ

new manager Grady Little.

As they move forward into the new century, the Red Sox

Boston added speed and a sure glove to the lineup by signing outfielder Johnny Damon in **2002**.

continue to seek their first world championship since 1918. They've come heartbreakingly close so many times, losing the World Series in seven games in 1946, 1967, 1975, and 1986. Yet each new season brings hope to Boston's die-hard fans, who continue to believe that

the Curse of the Bambino will soon be broken.

JOHNNY DAMON